Granny's GUIDE TO MARRIAGE IN VERSE

Wisdom for Brides

Practical applications are in poetic form.
Prayers and Scriptures are included.
All are from my personal experiences.

by Jean E. Oathout

GRANNY'S GUIDE TO MARRIAGE IN VERSE :
WISDOM FOR BRIDES
BY JEAN E. OATHOUT
Published by Lighthouse Publishing of the Carolinas
2333 Barton Oaks Dr., Raleigh, NC, 27614

ISBN 978-1-938499-99-9

Cover design by Ted Ruybal, www.wisdomhousebooks.com
Book design by Anna O'Brien www.behindthegift.com

Available in print from your local bookstore, online, or from the publisher at: www.lighthousepublishingofthecarolinas.com

For more information on this book and the author visit:
www.facebook.com/jean.oathout
www.twitter.com/#!/jeanoathout

Library of Congress Cataloging-in-Publication Data
Oathout, Jean E., Granny's Guide to Marriage in Verse: Wisdom for Brides / Jean E. Oathout.— 1st ed.

Printed in the United States of America

Table of Contents

Part 1
Granny's Guide to Marriage in Verse

Part 2:
My Personal Story

Acknowledgements

Those who helped me with suggestions to improve my book are Mary Huckle, MaryAnne Martin, Susan Blewett, Ann Mackey, Pat Wall, Nancy Sterniak, and Kathy Eastmond.

These friends have been a great help in guiding me in the presentation of the messages in my poems. I am deeply grateful for their help. I thank you, ladies.

I also value my grandson Benjamin Hull's expertise and all he did to help me understand how to use my computer for preparing the manuscripts. Without his help, I could not have accomplished all the Lord has asked me to do. Thank you, Ben.

Most of all, I thank the Lord for enabling me to accomplish this project. I look forward to learning how the e-book has helped other women find God's answers for themselves.

Jean E. Oathout

Testimonies/Endorsements

"Most books of poetry are tiresome, with trite phrasing and no central theme. Jean's work is a refreshing difference, with a clear, thematic devotional structure and wording that is original without being obscure. Best of all, she infuses her verses with strong biblical teaching, which makes for a rewarding devotional experience. Take a look --- you'll be hooked!"

David E. Fessenden, senior editor, CLC Publications • author of *Writing the Christian Nonfiction Book: Concept to Contract*

"I can't tell you enough how many changes I have recently seen in my husband and our marriage, since starting to read these poems and praying...along with taking some of the advice and quieting my mouth when I need to."

Kylie J., mother and housewife

"Jean's poems have personally touched and taught me! Thank you, Jean, for being obedient to God and for sharing your blessing with me! I like the personal feeling! These poems brought tears to my eyes! Great advice! Wow! Did you write these for me? Ouch, back in the 'refinery' I go! I have much more respect for my husband now!"

Mary H., mother, housewife, and nurse

"I am glad to recommend Jean's ministry of poetry. As you reflect on the message of these poems, you will encounter the Holy Spirit's presence in fresh, new ways."

Dennis King, pastor, Owego (NY) Church of the Nazarene

"I was flabbergasted to open Jean's volume and read these instructive devotional poems. What a variety of topics! What practical counsel! I hope these poems will bless many as they have impressed me."

Bob Hostetler, speaker, and author of 27 books

Granny's Guide to Marriage in Verse is the perfect engagement or personal wedding treasure for a bride. Jean Oathoat shares through sweet and tender poems the deep truths of married life. I felt like I was listening to a fairy godmother whispering poetic words of wisdom to the Princess bride. A precious book a bride will return to throughout married life and one day pass down to her children.

Elaine W. Miller, Speaker and Author of three books including, *We All Married Idiots: Three Things You'll Never Change About Your Life and Ten Things You Can.*

"Solid Biblical teaching on the topic of marriage is broken down into easily comprehended poems which give a thought to chew on in a day. The quotes and Bible verses at the end of the devotional are also thought provoking. Great for brides of any age."

Cleo Lampos, speaker, educator, author, *Teachers in the Trenches* and *Grandpa's Remembering Book.*

"Jean's poem are filled with practical advice that comes straight from the heart. Grounded in the truth of God's Word, she faithfully describes the beauty of a marriage between two people committed to each other and to God."

Barbara Warren, author of *The Gathering Storm*

"Those who enjoy poetry but who wouldn't read a how-to-do-marriage book will delight in Jean Oathout's tender encouragement and wisdom. Refresh your spirit and renew your love as you read *So You Want to Marry a Man.*"

Jeanette Levellie, Author, *Two Scoops of Grace with Chuckles on Top*

Foreword

After I'd written a journal of some of my experiences living with my husband in Vermont, I had a dream. I was in a room by myself, getting dressed. There happened to be a spotlight on me, and since it irritated me, I walked over and shut it off. When I did, I heard a woman in another room call out, "Hey! Who turned the light off?"

Shutting off the light in the dream made me realize that I should not quit. If I walked away from my present circumstances, many women would not benefit from the lessons I learned by doing things God's way in daily living as a wife and mother.

I believe God wanted me to use the journal I'd written and put it in poetic form. My mother had written many poems, so using her style was fairly easy for me.

I've arranged the poems in a 31-day devotional format. Each day's entry includes a related Scripture and a short prayer that will help the reader apply the poem's message. Hopefully, the poems will appeal to women who appreciate an older Christian woman's viewpoint on preparing for marriage, being married, and dealing with children in effective ways. My personal testimony is also included in this volume in 14 additional devotions.

In what I have shared, I bear witness to the fact that *real life* and true guidance are found in God's Word.

Jean E. Oathout

Preface

Any and all parts of this book
Were written down for you.
It is my prayer that as you look
You'll find things *you* can do.

My various poems surely tell
Of how it went with me.
As you will read I know quite well
Your own life you may see.

What I have found I want to share
To now enrich *your* life.
Maybe you'll find some answers there
That'll help *you* as a wife.

Our God will guide us so we can
To His great love relate.
I'm hopeful you will understand
He'll help *you* love your mate.

Some Scriptures are after each part,
So take time to read them.
It would be best to take to heart
Each message they will send.

In my book may God show *His* way
To help you with your need.
Please let Him guide you through each day
As these pages you read.

This book was a challenge for me.
I've tried to do my best.
It is my hope that you will be
Encouraged, helped, and blessed.

I've never written poems before
And perhaps it may show.
But please let them open a door
So faith in God can grow.

I've found from His inspiration
And guidance in my life,
We all have an obligation
To *learn* to be a wife.

Each time you read from this book
May you feel God is near.
I trust you'll find each day you look
That God's way is made clear.

I dedicate this book to you
The one who reads it now.
May you sense hope and guidance, too
To understand *your* vow.

As you search God's Word you will find
The way you are to live.
Single or married keep in mind
The answers God *will* give.

To put it simply,
marriage is a relationship
far more engrossing than we want it to be.
It always turns out to be more than we bargained for.
It is disturbingly intense,
disruptively involving,
and that is exactly how God designed it to be.

Mike Mason
The Mystery of Marriage

Part 1

Granny's Guide to Marriage in Verse

1

So You Plan to Marry

So you plan to marry—
A noble thing to do.
Be sure that you learn all you can
Of help there is for you.

The Bible has a lot to say
About this life you'll choose.
Be sure you're ready for that day
As single life you'll lose.

Humble yourself to God until
You have learned of His plan.
As you submit all of your will
God's way you'll understand.

If you have a spirit that's kind
God has blessings in store.
For former ways you'll stop but find
You'll learn there's so much more.

When you and your man are married
God sees you both as one.
It's hoped *self-will* you have buried
In your preparation.

Start now to trust in your man's care
So you'll *become* a team.
May you remember God is there
And on *Him* you can lean.

Take good counsel and accept correction—
that's the way to live wisely and well.
Proverbs 19:20 (MSG)

Father, I trust that I *will* listen to good advice.
Amen.

Marriage is not 50-50.
It is 100-100.
That way, the marriage always wins.
And when the marriage wins,
both spouses win.

Linda Wood Rondeau

2

It Is with Love I'm Writing Now

It is with love I'm writing now
To help you in your walk.
As you read this may you allow
The Lord to guide our talk.

Throughout the years it has been true
God's helped me through each day.
I'm confident He'll guide you too
So *you* can learn His way.

It's true folks look for help my dear
But some have never heard,
They'll find the answers are so near;
They're all found in God's Word.

Consider guidelines you'll receive
So His help you *will* find.
You'll see He wants you to believe
Through all these words of mine.

I hope you will become aware
Of what it can all mean.
You'll find it's true I long to share
That God's plan I have seen.

Together as we seek God's face
To learn what *He wants* done,
May you find by His wondrous grace
Your plans and His are one.

**Some trust in chariots, and some in horses;
But we will remember the name of the
LORD our God.
Psalm 20:7**

**Father, I ask that we seek *Your* will for us.
Amen.**

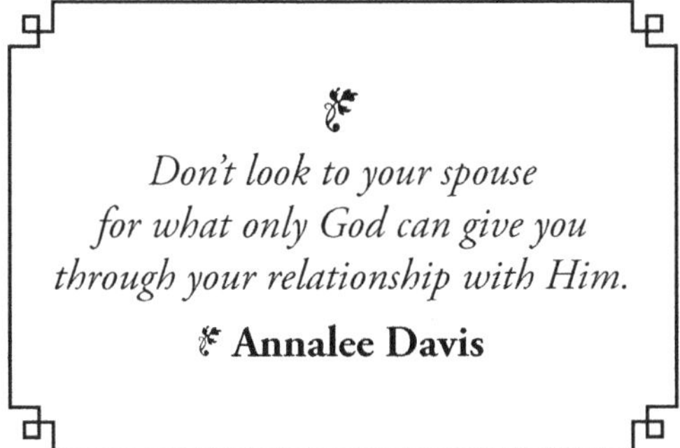
*Don't look to your spouse
for what only God can give you
through your relationship with Him.*
Annalee Davis

3

It's True Our God Has Made Creatures

It's true our God has made creatures;
He had a plan in mind.
He gave each one special features
And made them like *their* kind.

The man's not meant to be forlorn
Or feel that he's the least.
For God has plans for each one born
And it includes each beast.

The woman needs purpose in life
To find out *why* she'll live.
Is it she'll *plan* to be a wife?
Commitments to it give?

If there's no marriage in God's sight
And there's no vow to stay,
To live together is not right
For it is *not* God's way.

Because He's Love, God takes the task
To help them understand,
It's His design that love should last
For the woman and man.

The question is will they commit
Their love and energy?
Will each agree that they'll submit
To what *God* wants to be?

God said, "It is not good for the man to be alone; I'll make him a helper, a companion....God used the rib that he had taken from the man to make woman and presented her to the man."
Genesis 2:18a, 22 (MSG)

Father, help me make good decisions for my life. Amen.

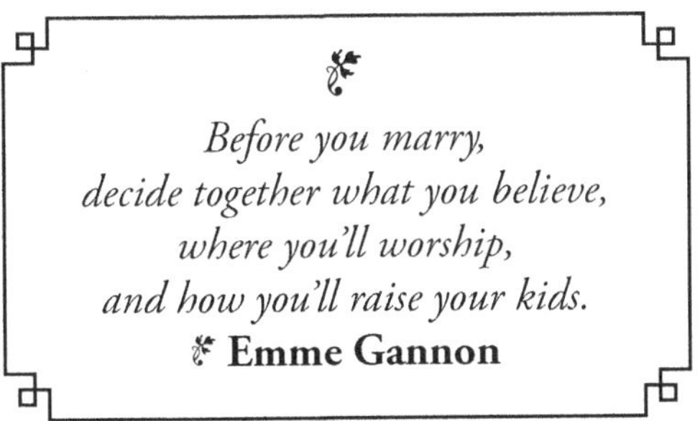

4

You'll Need to Know What Is God's View

You'll need to know what is God's view
And just what His Word states.
He'll help you with some guidelines too
To keep you from mistakes.

Right now it's true you're *free* to choose
To live single or not.
Remember, *singleness you lose*
When a husband you've got.

It's important to look within
To be sure he's the one.
In time to come you'll marry him;
It will be said and done.

There will be freedoms as a wife
You hadn't known before.
They're meant to last through your whole life
And bless you with much more.

God wants husbands to learn to be
The ones who are to lead.
They are to have *authority*
To guide in every need.

The Lord will tutor them along.
The way is in His Book.
He wants to help them to be strong
If in His Word they'll look.

. . .I am the LORD your God, who teaches you to profit, who leads you by the way you should go.
Isaiah 48:17b

Father, may we find the way that pleases You. Amen.

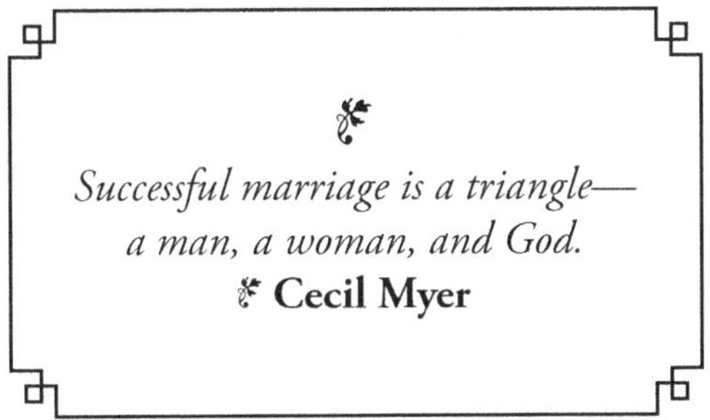

Successful marriage is a triangle—
a man, a woman, and God.
Cecil Myer

5

We Are to Put God First in Life

We are to put God first in life
And in Him we're to trust.
Our husbands next when we're a wife
And what *they* ask of us.

Open God's Word and you will read
Some clear-cut guidelines there.
Submit to Him so He can lead
And prove that He does care.

God's will for you can become clear
In what He will want done.
You'll find He is so very near—
The Omnipresent One.

Your own obedience will bring
What God desires to be.
You'll learn His way to do a thing
Is what you are to see.

The Lord wants us to serve others
For our *real* happiness.
One's selfishness is what smothers
As it can bring distress.

May we remember God's *right* way
Is for *our* very best.
It won't be easy to obey
But by it we'll be blessed.

Trust in Him at all times, you people;
Pour out your heart before Him;
God is a refuge for us. Selah.
Psalm 62:8

Father, enable me to trust in You.
Amen.

Marriage is not a noun; it's a verb.
It isn't something you get.
It's something you do—
You love your partner every day.

Barbara DeAngelis

6

Lord Jesus Came and Gave His Life

Lord Jesus came and gave His life
So God's love we can know.
As you may someday be a wife
He'll help *your* love to grow.

In all our souls God's placed a part
That *craves* His tender love.
It was created in each heart
To find this love above.

As God will wait right near you there
To help you through each day,
You'll find that He is everywhere
And hears you when you pray.

Just bow your head and ask Christ in.
His love to you He'll give.
With resurrection power within
He'll come inside to live.

When God can rule *priorities*
And in Him we will trust,
We'll find that it's revealed He sees
And knows what's *best* for us.

It makes no difference the test
But how we do *react.*
With God's help may you give your best
And sense it as a fact.

The Lord is my strength and my shield; My heart trusted in Him, and I am helped.
Psalm 28:7a

Father, please be *my* strength and shield.
Amen.

You can never be happily married
to another until you get
a divorce from yourself!
Successful marriage demands
a certain death to self.
Jerry McCant

7

Maybe It's True You've Not Been Shown

Maybe it's true you've not been shown
Just what God's love can mean.
And could it be you've never known
Your need which you've not seen?

You may think you are quite okay
By your *"good living"* now.
You don't know Jesus is *The Way*
And to Him you're to bow.

The Lord with love *your* sins did take
And hung them on His cross.
His mission He did not forsake
Or we'd be at great loss.

Christ's blood was there for us outpoured
For punishment of sin.
Some folks believed but some ignored
What all it *did cost* Him.

Into the grave His body went.
He took our sin and shame.
It is for this that He was sent;
Because of love He came.

He rose again that we might live
And have *New Life* inside.
To us we now have found He'll give
His Spirit to abide.

For God so loved the world that He gave His only begotten Son, that whoever believes in Him should not perish but have everlasting life.
John 3:16

Father, I believe in Jesus. Please forgive *my* sins! Amen.

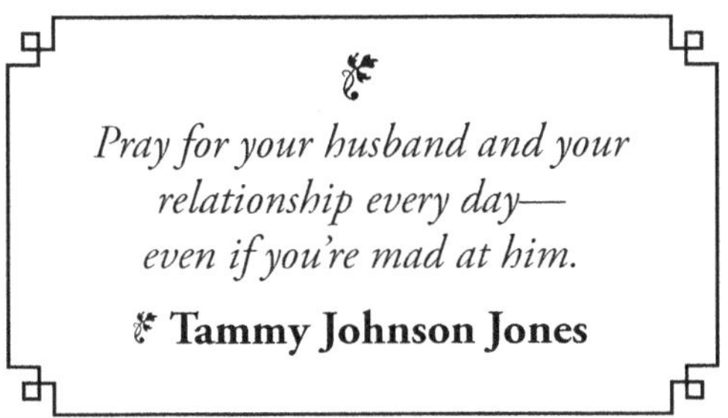

Pray for your husband and your relationship every day— even if you're mad at him.

Tammy Johnson Jones

8

The Road Gets Rough When Two Wills Meet

The road gets rough when two wills meet
As each one wants *his* way.
It's hoped that God's plan they will seek
And His Word they'll obey.

Our God through Christ does understand
What we are going through.
You'll find it's true *He* was a man
And walked in flesh like *you*.

This Jesus knows that you are there.
He'll hear *your* every cry.
He has a heart that's full of care
To answer every "*Why?*"

God's promises we are to find
Are true and what will last.
We are to learn that He is kind
But *waits* for us to ask.

As you pour out your heart to Him
And read His Holy Word,
Allow His Spirit to come in
So His voice can be heard.

Through faith in Christ God leads us on
To show the way to go.
For we have found that God's Own Son
Can see us here below.

Out of respect for Christ,
be courteously reverent to one another.
Ephesians 5:21 (MSG)

Father, help us learn *Your ways* for our marriage.
Amen.

Forgive a lot.
Forget even more.

Debbie Banks

9

God Will Reveal from Time to Time

God will reveal from time to time
The thing that we will hide.
It's for our good if we can find
To take it in our stride.

As God will look into your heart
To know what's hidden there,
You'll find He can take it apart
And open it up bare.

To have His love to come in you
You'll need to *clear* the way.
Your bitterness and anger too
Are things that cannot stay.

You are to deal with what you see
And face them as a fact.
You'll overcome, have victory
If you will not *react.*

Confess to God you understand
When once you see *your* need.
Ask Jesus now to take command
So that you can be freed.

You'll find God's love begins to flow
As hindrances do leave.
Study His Word so you will know
His Spirit you won't grieve.

That the God of our Lord Jesus Christ, the Father of glory, may give to you the spirit of wisdom and revelation in the knowledge of Him.
Ephesians 1:17

Father, I see I need *Your* wisdom and knowledge. Amen.

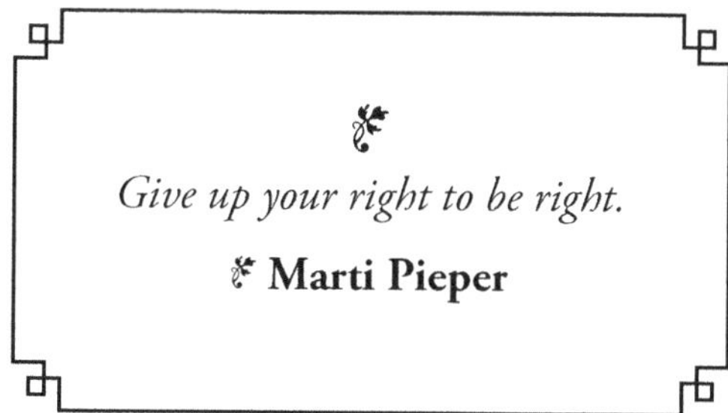

Give up your right to be right.

Marti Pieper

10

God's Presence You Can Know Right Here

God's Presence you can know right here
And His love you *can* feel.
It may sometimes bring on a tear
As with you He will deal.

The holiness of God you'll see
As you repent of sin.
You'll understand you're not worthy
His Presence to be in.

Salvation for you is to come
When on Jesus you call.
The Spirit's *seal* on you is done
As peace on you will fall.

Invite Him in to be in charge
And surrender your life.
His love will prove to be quite large
To help you as a wife.

Be confident that He *will* lead
When more of God you know.
With hunger now you are to feed
On His Word so you'll grow.

God's gentle and He's peaceable
But He will wait on you.
Open your heart. Be teachable.
His ways to follow through.

Seek the Lord while He may be found,
call upon Him while He is near.
Isaiah 55:6

Father, I desire Your Spirit to fill me *now*.
Amen.

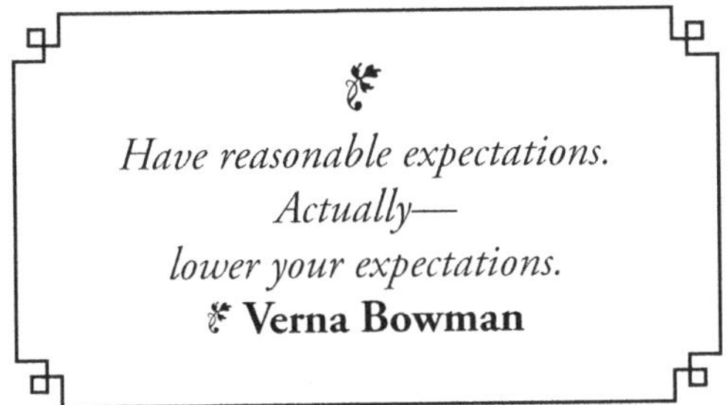

Have reasonable expectations.
Actually—
lower your expectations.
Verna Bowman

11

When You Surrender *All* Your Life

When You surrender *all* your life
To Jesus Christ the King,
He'll be your Guide when you're a wife
And all that it can bring.

There'll be some days when *nothin's* right;
It seems that God's not there.
But chances are you have *lost sight*
For God is *everywhere.*

There is no place where you can hide
For God will know your need.
Be confident that He can guide
And trust He'll gently lead.

Our God will give inspiration
You'll find throughout the years.
It's how we'll learn the relation
Of softened wills and tears.

As the Bible will clearly tell
God's thoughts for you each day,
He wants to help you answer well
Whatever comes your way.

The thing that God will have you do
Won't be too hard to find.
For He will always be near you
No matter what the bind.

I will say of the LORD, "He is my refuge and my fortress; My God, in Him I will trust."
Psalm 91:2

Father, help me remember that *You* are my refuge. Amen.

Take care of each other in the good times so you'll know how to take care of each other in the bad times.

Sarah Burns Hampshire

12

Receive God's Love So Others Know

Receive God's Love so others know
You live for His glory.
For it is true your faith *will* show
When God's way others see.

You'll find God knows your deepest care
And hears each word you say.
May you discover He's right there
And longs to *show* His way.

It is with love He reaches out
To draw you to Himself.
He will reveal your every doubt
Begins *within* yourself.

God's Word says He has made some plans
To help you to succeed.
He knows your needs and understands
And hears each time you plead.

May you be touched with His great love
So you can give your best.
His Grace will come from up above.
It's yours at your request.

You'll find God has ways for us wives
To bring us dividends.
In time we'll have satisfied lives
But on *us* it depends.

For I know the thoughts that I think toward you, saith the LORD, thoughts of peace, and not of evil, to give you an expected end.
Jeremiah 29:11 (KJV)

Father, I ask for Your thoughts for me.
Amen.

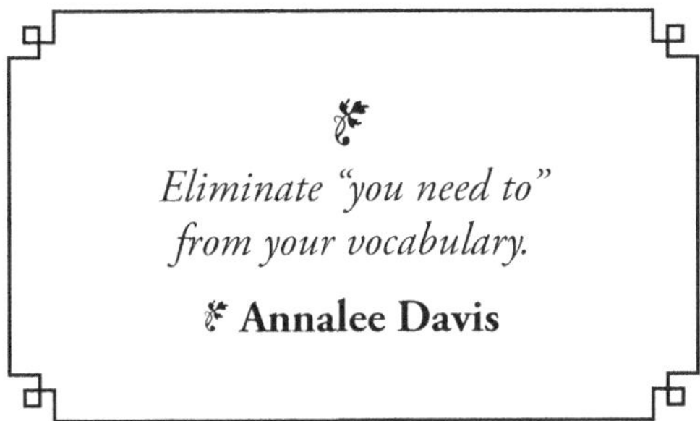

Eliminate "you need to" from your vocabulary.

Annalee Davis

13

Too Often the Mouth Speaks of Faith

Too often the mouth speaks of faith
Before the actions tell.
It seems to be that some can't wait.
Their faith they try to sell.

Have faith unto yourself and see
That others will soon know,
You have true Christianity
For Christ's love you will show.

When we trust our man with our life
Our *faith* goes along too.
When *you* start to live as a wife
May Christ's love come through you.

As Jesus wants to be the guide
For you and your husband,
He'll cause your faith to grow *inside*
So you can love your man.

Your faith will need encouragement
Through all the years to come.
To go to church is important
So seek God for *which* one.

There may be times you can't get there
So know this in advance,
God understands and He's aware
You'll go at any chance.

Let the words of my mouth and the meditation of my heart be acceptable in Your sight, O LORD, my strength and my Redeemer.
Psalm 19:14

Father, help me be careful of what I say.
Amen.

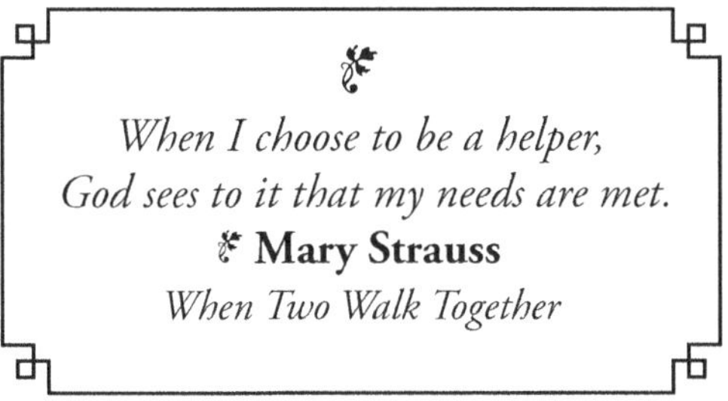

When I choose to be a helper,
God sees to it that my needs are met.
Mary Strauss
When Two Walk Together

14

What Will You *Now* Plan for Your Life

What will you *now* plan for your life
To benefit mankind?
If you have plans to be a wife
Some guidance you will find.

Don't take it lightly 'cause you'll see
A lot depends on you.
Your husband's "other half" you'll be.
You'll be a team of *two*.

It's best for your husband to *lead*.
You are to *support* him.
You will discover you've a need
To change some things *within*.

To learn this it may take some time
For your will to remake.
Allow God's Word to help your mind
To see it's for *your* sake.

As it's God's will to show you how
To make it through it all,
He will make it become clear now,
For His help you're to call.

Your faith will help you every day
So you can carry on.
God's Word will tell you what to say
So His peace may be won.

Every wise woman builds her house,
but the foolish pulls it down with her hands.
Proverbs 14:1

Father, I ask You to guide my life.
Amen.

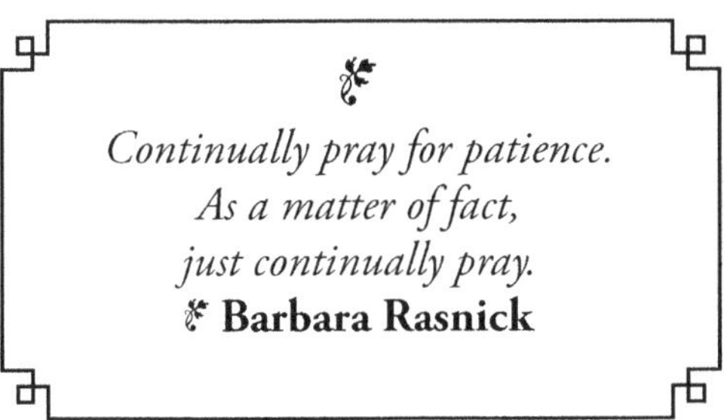

Continually pray for patience.
As a matter of fact,
just continually pray.
Barbara Rasnick

15

Christ Longs for You His Word to Read

Christ longs for you His Word to read
So His way you will know.
It is His Word you are to heed
That by it you can grow.

Your life depends on what *you do*
As time your footsteps fill.
You'll find it is given to you
To live just as you will.

As God is Love He'll make it clear
He wants to share this love.
His Voice He longs for you to hear
As softly as a dove.

His promises to you He'll keep
As you now claim each one.
Your deep devotion He will seek
When each new day is done.

You'll find to Him you'll bring *glory*
As you walk in His Way.
Your life will become *His story*
When on His path you stay.

He sees the hunger in your heart
To stand up to this test.
In time you'll learn what is *your* part
As in His love you rest.

Ponder the path of your feet, And let all your ways be established. Do not turn to the right or to the left; Remove your foot from evil.
Proverbs 4:26-27

Father, may I faithfully call on You for help.
Amen.

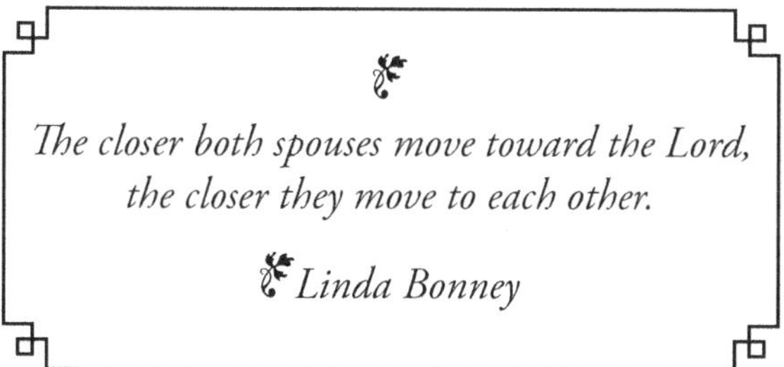

16

If You Have Faith You *Can* Make It

If you have faith you *can* make it;
At times you may feel "down,"
So ask God to help you *take it*
And wipe away your frown.

We are to pray when life seems tough
For Jesus to guide us.
We'll find that He will be *enough*
When in Him we do trust.

As we're not promised many days
Or that a year we'll live,
It's best we find out some new ways
Each day our love to give.

As you surrender to God's will
You'll learn about His love.
May it be you'll listen until
His thoughts come from above.

It's God Who'll give you guidance, dear
So that you can soon see,
How you're to live will become clear
In each adversity.

When on God's Word folks see you stand
You'll find *they* can be blessed.
You will help them to know God's plan
To guide them in *their* test.

Cast thy burden upon the Lord, and He shall sustain thee: he shall never suffer the righteous to be moved.
Psalm 55:22 (KJV)

Father, with Your help I can overcome anything. Amen.

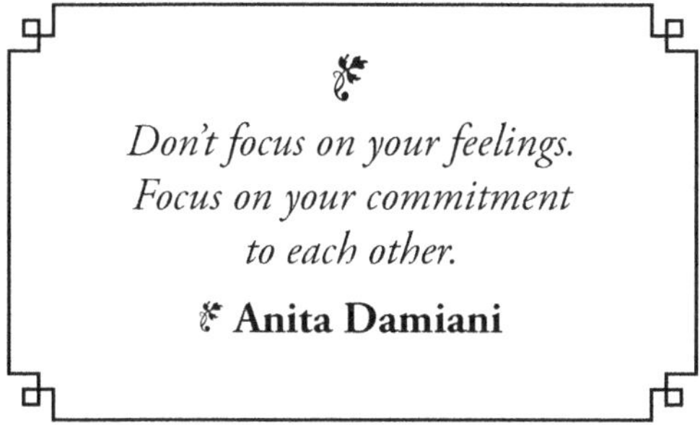

Don't focus on your feelings.
Focus on your commitment
to each other.

Anita Damiani

17

It Does Take Time for Faith to Grow

It does take time for faith to grow
And troubles help it too.
You'll find God guides you as you go
For He longs to bless you.

What you'll discover as a wife
It's not now understood.
But Jesus will work in your life
To benefit *your* good.

If you can learn to be thankful
And take what comes your way,
You'll see that when you are grateful
It helps you *through* each day.

Our God won't push or shove at all
But waits instead to hear
A person like yourself who'll call
And *want* His Presence near.

Lord Jesus is the name we use;
It is the name God gave.
His Word does say He won't refuse
A call on Him to save.

Christ's *peace* will come to you right there
If you'll but ask Him in.
You'll know release from every care
When *His Life* comes within.

**Therefore, having been justified by faith,
we have peace with God through our
Lord Jesus Christ.
Romans 5:1**

**Father, I want this peace to be mine.
Amen.**

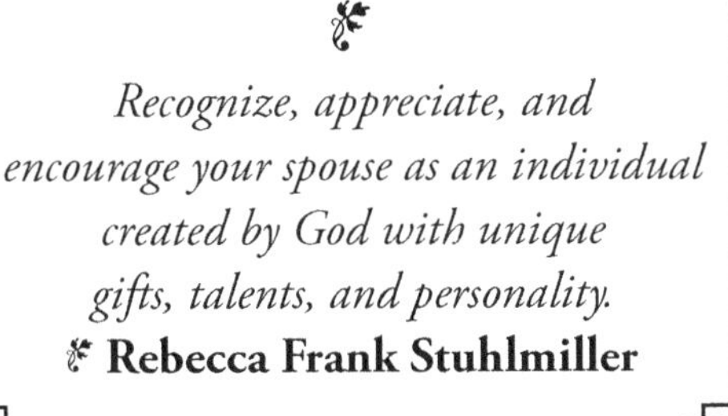

*Recognize, appreciate, and
encourage your spouse as an individual
created by God with unique
gifts, talents, and personality.*
Rebecca Frank Stuhlmiller

18

You'll Need to Have a Private Time

You'll need to have a private time
To be with God alone.
As you are quiet you will find
The time you'll not bemoan.

Each day as you take time to talk
With God through Christ in prayer,
You'll learn He'll guide you in your walk
Each time you meet Him there.

As He will gently show the way
When time for Him you set,
Before the "hurry" of the day
His guidance you're to get.

If your desire is now to learn
To do the best you can,
It's to God's Word you'll need to turn
For *help* to love your man.

In Psalms the prayers help you start
For they'll express your cry.
When you pray them you will take heart
As God's Word you'll apply.

To find out *how* to be a mate
God's plan you'll need to know.
As you become quite still and wait,
In time His way He'll show.

For the eyes of the LORD are on the righteous,
And His ears are open to their prayers…
1 Peter 3:12a

Father, draw me close to You so that I may
know you intimately.
Amen.

Make him feel special—
or someone else will!
Karen Katramados

19

Lord, Help Me Show Your Love Today

Lord, help me show Your love today
In everything I do.
Please help me watch the words I say
So they may all *please* You.

I'm glad You care so much for me
And that You know *my* need.
Open my eyes so I may see
The way *You* want to lead.

Please help me know that there is some
Good help which can be found.
I realize the time has come
To get advice that's sound.

I can now see that as a wife
I'll need to read Your Book.
Please help me dedicate my life
As in Your Word I look.

Because I want to give my best
Your help I know I'll win.
I will desire to pass this test
And let You reign within.

I trust my attitudes will change
And make a difference.
I pray that You will rearrange
My total inner sense.

Then I will give them one heart, and I will put a new spirit within them, and take the stony heart out of their flesh, and give them a heart of flesh.
Ezekiel 11:19

Father, give me this *new heart* You speak of here.
Amen.

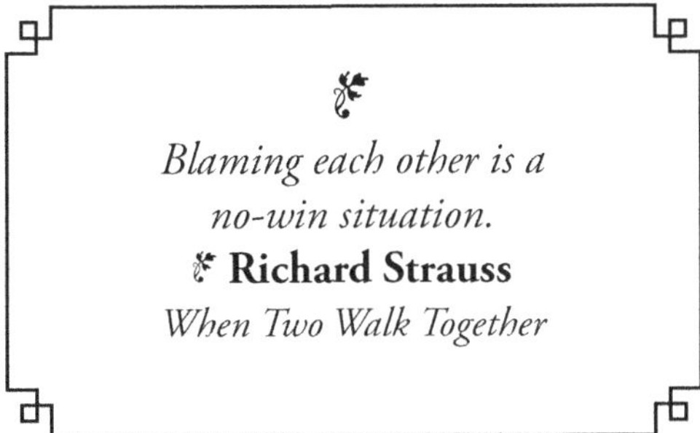

Blaming each other is a
no-win situation.
Richard Strauss
When Two Walk Together

20

It Would Be Good to Have Some Talks

It would be good to have some talks
And learn each other's dreams.
Maybe you'll need to go on walks
And stroll beneath moonbeams.

For sure you will become aware
That from the very start,
There will be things you'll need to share
Which weigh upon *your* heart.

When on a walk you plan to go
Do let him set the pace.
If you don't step in front you'll show
That trust in him you place.

In this time as you walk with him
How you feel will come out.
It may reveal some thoughts within
Which have caused you some doubt.

It's true our mouths cause us trouble
When God's ways we've not tried.
As we repent on the double
We let God work *inside.*

The Lord can help your man to see
His thoughts you want to seek.
As you try to listen you'll be
Ready to hear him speak.

Wherefore, my beloved brethren, let every man be swift to hear, slow to speak, slow to wrath.
James 1:19 (KJV)

Father, help us learn to communicate well.
Amen.

Don't keep secrets from each other.
Fran Pasch

21

Try Riding Backwards in a Car

Try riding backwards in a car
With your man at the wheel.
It will be hard to go too far
No backward glance to steal.

Your man needs you to learn to trust
And in his judgments rest.
To trust him now becomes a must
So he will try his best.

When you are lost or it does seem
Don't be too quick to speak.
Directions may be what he'll deem
And be what he should seek.

Your lives he'll also try to steer
So let him think things through.
You'll find in time he'll want to hear
An opinion from you.

So when you think you know life's way
That both of you should go,
Be very careful what you say
And your *respect* to show.

Because God made your man to be
A *leader* in advance,
He'll make decisions you will see
If given half a chance.

Teach me good judgment and knowledge,
For I believe Your commandments.
Psalm 119:66

Father, help me trust in my husband's decisions.
Amen.

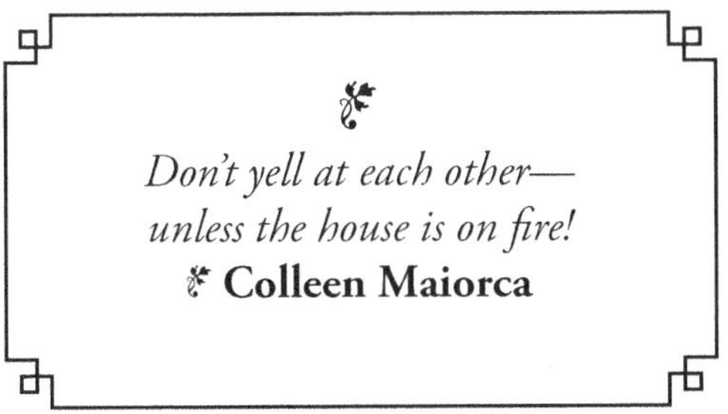

Don't yell at each other—
unless the house is on fire!
Colleen Maiorca

22

Sometimes You'll Not Know *What* to Say

Sometimes you'll not know *what* to say
Or what you are to do.
You'll find you cannot know the way
As you are blinded too.

When God can control everything
You will soon understand,
That your commitment is to bring
A chance to *help* your man.

To know that Jesus does show care
When you call on *His* name,
Will help you to believe to where
Your life won't be the same.

Pray too that you will touch Christ's heart
Each time your need is great.
You'll find He's faithful in *His* part
And guides you for *your* sake.

As you seek God's Face you will see
He'll help you to endure.
The plans He has for you will be
What's best for you I'm sure.

His promises will help you grow
To learn what love's about.
Whatever God will bid you know
His way you *can* find out.

The righteous cry out, and the LORD hears,
And delivers them out of all their troubles.
Psalm 34:17

Father, I sure need Your help to know what to say.
Amen.

What counts in making
a happy marriage is not so much how
compatible you are,
but how you deal with incompatibility.
Leo Tolstoy

23

A Lady Once Waited for Strength

A lady once waited for strength
To do what God told her.
She asked the Lord at some great length
To make her courage stir.

She was dismayed it never came
To help her with this task.
Next time she found it was the same.
She faithfully did ask.

As she wanted the Lord to please
And try her very best,
She humbly went upon her knees
For help to pass this test.

When she remembered what was told
She was obedient.
To her delight God made her bold
To go where she was sent.

So you'll find too that when you try
To obey what you've heard,
He will reveal the reason why
You'll need to heed His Word.

When you step out in faith you'll see
And start to understand,
That God will help you as you be
Submissive to your man.

And whatsoever you do, do it heartily,
as to the Lord and not unto men.
Colossians 3:23 (KJV)

Father, please enable me to be cooperative.
Amen.

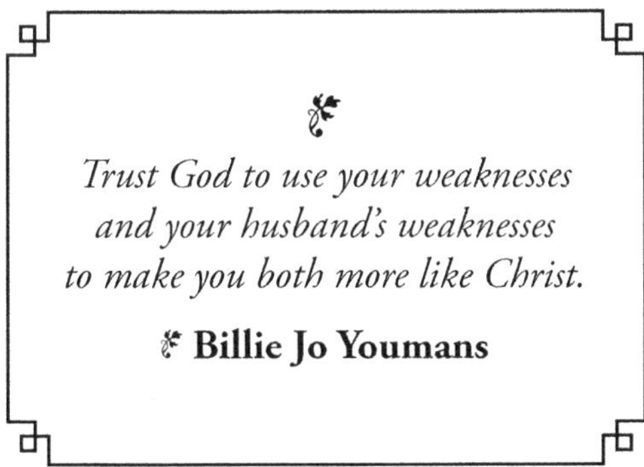

Trust God to use your weaknesses
and your husband's weaknesses
to make you both more like Christ.

Billie Jo Youmans

24

We're to Submit to Find Our Rest

We're to submit to find our rest
In each adversity.
For God will help us in our test
And be there faithfully.

When married you'll be a "help mate"
To be of *help* to him.
With your husband will you relate
And keep your peace within?

As you look close you'll see the fact
That some resentments flare,
When you at times find you react
To hurts you weren't aware.

Why did it *irritate* you so?
And why were you upset?
Why does it seem to you as though
Your way just must be met?

When you're tempted to be hateful
Stop—get away alone.
As God helps you to be grateful
You'll see His grace you've known.

"I told you so" should not be said
When things go as they may.
So *pray* your man will learn instead
To handle things God's way.

He who hates, disguises it with his lips,
And lays up deceit within himself.
Proverbs 26:24

Father, I don't want to be hateful.
Help me to *pray* instead.
Amen.

Keep thy eyes wide open before marriage, and half-shut afterwards.

Thomas Fuller

25

The "*Lovin*" You May Both Do Now

The "*lovin*" you may both do now
Before you two marry,
Will rob blessings for you somehow
And guilt you will carry.

The more you kiss and touch and feel
The more you will lose out.
You'll find some future joy you'll steal
As it can cause a drought.

"Experimental love" cheapens
The love that's *meant to be.*
In time you'll sense that it deepens
And mature love you'll see.

The *marriage bed* is undefiled
And meant for our pleasure.
Now that you've grown and aren't a child
It's to become a treasure.

You'll find you *can* give to your mate
A love that is *untried.*
It's to your benefit to wait
Until the "knot is tied."

You'll give yourself to your husband
On that *eventful day.*
Trust God to help you so you can
Commit to him to stay.

. . .But God is faithful, Who will not allow you to be tempted beyond what you are able, but with the temptation will also make the way of escape. . .
1 Corinthians 10:13b

Father, please help me be discreet in all I allow. Amen.

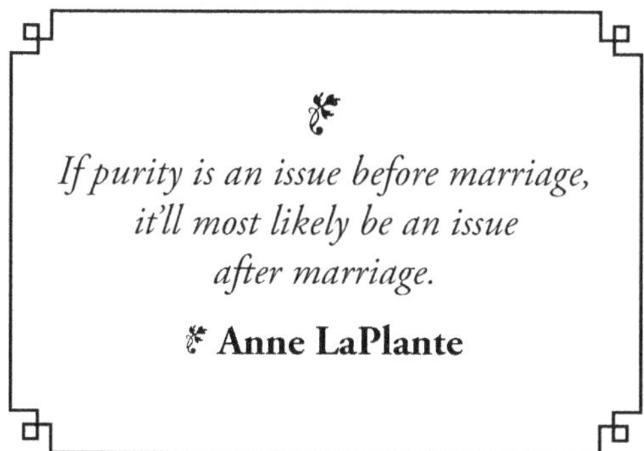

If purity is an issue before marriage, it'll most likely be an issue after marriage.

Anne LaPlante

26

Our God Will Want the Very Best

Our God will want the very best
For you when you're a wife.
Let *your* faith help you in this test
To guide you all through life.

The Word God gave to us will show
That He does surely care.
As He's aware He'll surely know
All burdens you will share.

When we desire the truth to see
From those who teach God's Word,
We'll check their words more carefully
To see if *Truth* we've heard.

It won't take long for you to learn
If your soul *they* should feed.
You'll understand if they can earn
The right for them to lead.

It's when you desire to be wise
You will *discern* God's way.
So prayerfully now recognize
God's Word for you each day.

As God is love He'll help you stand
Behind His Word that's true.
In time you'll find you really *can*
Follow God's will for you.

...Believe in the LORD your God,
and you shall be established; believe His prophets,
and you shall prosper.
2 Chronicles 20:20b_

Father, lead me to those who teach *Your* Word.
Amen.

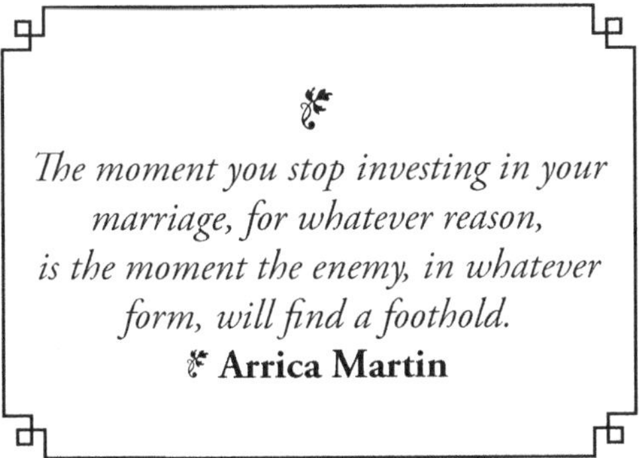

The moment you stop investing in your marriage, for whatever reason, is the moment the enemy, in whatever form, will find a foothold.
Arrica Martin

27

When Troubles Come into Your life

When troubles come into your life
You will want to know why.
The Lord will help you as a wife
To see it by and by.

Advice you will desire to give
That you feel is needed.
But it depends on how you live
Whether it is heeded.

You need to know God has a plan
To bless you in hard times.
Depend on Him to lead your man
And that His will he finds.

When you want God to speak to him
It's best to be quiet.
As God will lead him from within
Let him be led by it.

You'll find it's awesome as you see
That God *does* have a way,
To inspire your man so that *He*
Can tell him what to say.

When he decides what he will do
Don't make a suggestion.
Too late may be a word from you.
It may bring confusion.

Be merciful to me, O God, be merciful to me! For my soul trusts in you; And in the shadow your wings I will make my refuge, until these calamities have passed by.
Psalm 57:1

Father, You are my refuge. I trust in your wisdom. Amen.

Always be running for re-election as president of your husband's fan club.
Linda Bonney

28

Some Years of Marriage You May Find

Some years of marriage you may find
Can be hard ones for sure.
You're to recall and keep in mind
God helps us to endure.

It's true that God will meet our need
When His Word we have used.
You'll find that as you let Him lead
Your lives can both be fused.

He doesn't seem to care who calls
As long as *faith* is there.
When troubles come there'll be no walls
To block His love and care.

Our ways in which we trust dearly
We are to give to Him.
He'll help us learn *His* ways clearly
So peace *can* come within.

It's good to know that Christ loves you
And intercedes each day.
His peace and grace, gentleness too
Are with you all the way.

Remember as you travel on
Jesus is by your side.
He walks with you till life is done
And with you He'll abide.

. . .It is Christ who died, and furthermore is also risen, who is even at the right hand of God, who also makes intercession for us.
Romans 8:34

Father, I thank You that Christ intercedes for me. Amen.

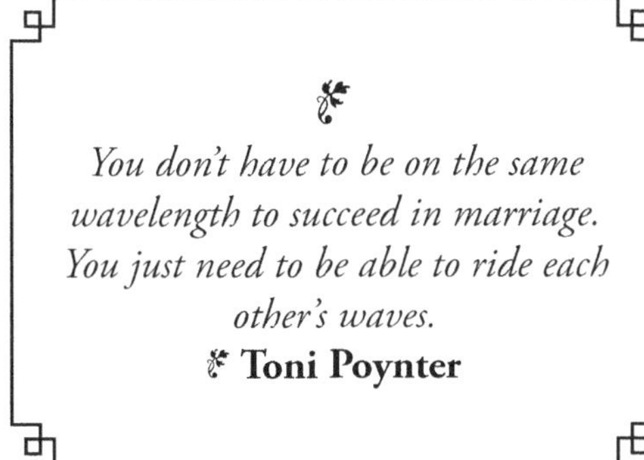

You don't have to be on the same wavelength to succeed in marriage. You just need to be able to ride each other's waves.
Toni Poynter

29

It's True That We Can Have Real Joy

It's true that we can have real joy
When we walk in God's way.
As righteous concepts we employ
And in His Word we stay.

What God has planned for both of you
In time you will be told.
Your future can be best with two
So let *God's* way unfold.

Now take a good look at your man
As you will try to dream.
You'll find you need to understand
And know what it *can* mean.

It's when your man sees submission
His love for you can grow.
You'll learn that from this relation
Your faith in God will show.

Do set a watch at your mouth's door.
Make it a daily cry.
Open your heart and ask for more
As on God you rely.

It's hoped good times will be enough
To help you clearly see,
That when the daily life gets rough
You'll *face* adversity.

A man has joy by the answer of his mouth,
And a word spoken in due season,
how good it is.
Proverbs 15:23

Father, help me to speak my words *carefully*.
Amen.

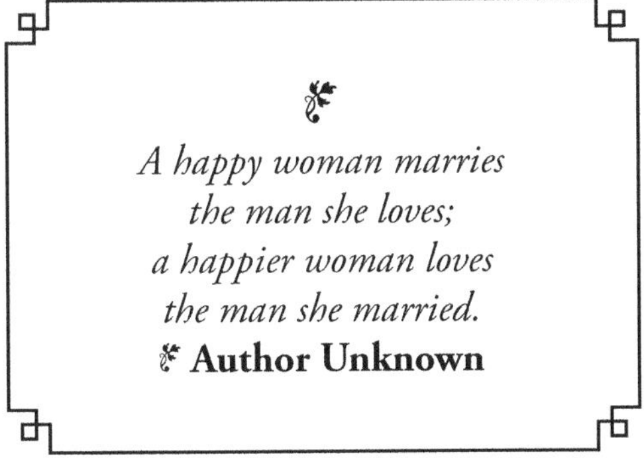

A happy woman marries
the man she loves;
a happier woman loves
the man she married.
Author Unknown

30

Be Sure You Live Each Day, My Friend

Be sure you live each day, my friend
To see what God will do.
Before you pray He's planned to send
His answers on to you.

Your prayer time is what God waits for
So His plan can be shown.
Requests will open up the door
For His way to be *known.*

Will you look always to the One
Who's called you by His voice?
It's in your hand what will be done.
God wants to hear *your* choice.

If you'll choose friends who *live* the life
And ones who *know* God's grace,
They'll wisely help you be a wife
To find what is *your* place.

You need to understand to get
Your burdened heart to sing,
You'll need to pray that you will let
What's *best* for Him to bring.

While you trust Christ for what it takes
To change you *and* your man,
May you stay true for *both* your sakes
So that your faith will stand.

**But without faith it is impossible to please Him,
for he who comes to God must believe that He is,
and that He is a rewarder of those
who diligently seek Him.
Hebrews 11:6**

**Father, I see my need to *believe* that You can help us.
Amen.**

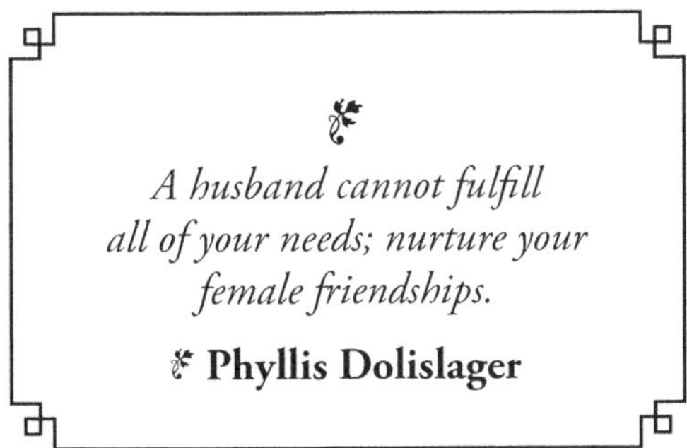

*A husband cannot fulfill
all of your needs; nurture your
female friendships.*

Phyllis Dolislager

31

My Heart Goes Out to You, My Dear

My heart goes out to you, my dear
As you will look ahead.
Some things may cause you now to fear
But please trust God instead.

When you give thought to what to do
Both now and later on,
Know that the Lord is there with you
To guide each decision.

The preparations are many
For you to be a bride.
It's best for you there aren't any
Surprises that may hide.

I trust these verses help you see
There's so much you can learn.
If you are ready you will be
Blessed with all you'll yearn.

Ask God to show on what to stand
And which way you're to go.
With a perspective of *His plan*
His will you both can know.

Commit yourself to God right now
And willingly obey.
As you read His Word you'll see how
It is for you today.

In whom we have boldness and access with confidence through faith in Him.
Ephesians 3:12

Father, may my life be an *example* of Your grace. Amen.

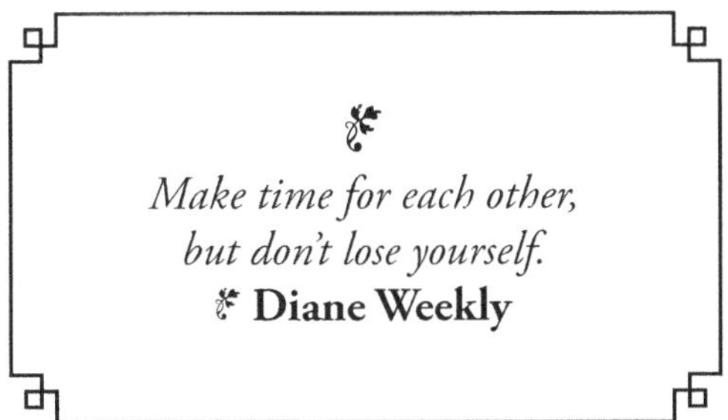

The will of God is never exactly what
you expect it to be.
It may seem to be much worse,
but in the end,
it's going to be much better.

Elisabeth Elliot

Part 2:

My Personal Story

1

The Vision That I Had One Day

The vision that I had one day;
The Lord stood by my side.
From childhood He would lead the way
And with me He'd abide.

And when a teen I prayed one night
For Christ to save my soul.
His Word would guide me to live right
So I would be made whole.

It's true that through my life I've sought
Some folks with *truth* to share.
To many questions I'd been taught;
The answers just weren't there.

Most every time I heard God's Word
The Scriptures I did search.
I tested each message I heard
Regardless of the church.

I'd felt *somewhere* Truth could be known
And would be shared with me.
I did long for it to be shown
And the Truth I could see.

I found some folks who weren't afraid
To share the Truth *they* had.
Because I was impressed I stayed.
Their worship made me glad.

**Fear not, for I am with you; Be not dismayed,
for I am your God. I will strengthen you,
Yes, I will help you,
I will uphold you with My righteous right hand.
Isaiah 41:10**

**Father, I'm thankful You heard my cry.
Amen.**

2

My Husband Knew I Was to Go

My husband knew I was to go
And to attend that night.
So off I went though I did know
There may well be a fight.

I didn't seem to understand
My husband was my head.
I did not submit to my man
But went my way instead.

As it was Truth from God I'm sure
God would have made a way.
My own desire no doubt was pure
But I *failed* to obey.

I'd been submissive to my mate
And had been a good wife.
But I did not know I should wait
And trust God with my life.

Later I found that in God's Word
He shows His plan for us.
As His way I had never heard
My marriage I did bust.

I prayed God would reveal to me
What next I was to do.
His plan I was to find to be
The course He'd guide me through.

For the husband is head of the wife,
as also Christ is head of the church;
and He is the Savior of the body.
Ephesians 5:23

Father, forgive me for failing to make
***good* decisions.**
Amen.

3

A *"Good Person"* I'd Tried to Be

A *"good person"* I'd tried to be
And obeyed truths I'd heard.
But there I felt that I could see
The *power* in God's Word.

The worship I saw looked so good;
I longed to try it too.
I felt awkward but knew I should
Join all I saw *them* do.

I was to see what they had learned
Opened my heart up wide.
I felt God's Presence and I yearned
For Him to come *inside.*

As others were baptized that night,
Young people and a man,
I knew God's Word I shouldn't fight.
I prayed to understand.

I sensed that God was truly there
As my eyes filled with tears.
I could now see that God *did* care.
He'd help me through *my* fears.

It was to the water I went.
I longed now to obey.
In heartfelt joy I did repent.
I knew it was *God's* way.

Whosoever is wise will observe these things, And they will understand the lovingkindness of the LORD.
Psalm 107:43

Father, I want to *obey* the truth I hear.
Amen.

4

I Began to Look Down Inside

I began to look down inside
My sinful self to see.
I asked God's Spirit to abide
And be a friend to me.

I learned my sin was buried now
By virtue of Christ's Name.
I soon began to notice how
My tongue He'd have to tame.

So on my knees I went each day
And spent some time in prayer.
'Twas evident I'd have to stay
And let God touch me there.

My children did a daily check
If the Spirit had come.
They wondered too if I would let
This inward work be done.

Heaven's language was what they heard;
God's Spirit came within.
I found He's true to His Own Word
When I *let* Him come in.

Although I'd gone to this new church
For only a short time,
I saw that my diligent search
Had made some more Truth *mine.*

And also on My menservants
and on My maidservants
I will pour out My Spirit in those days.
Joel 2:29

Father, thank You for Your *faithfulness* to me.
Amen.

5

I Gleaned from Others Day by Day

I gleaned from others day by day
And found that I desired,
To live for God in every way
As my faith was *inspired.*

God's Word I was to daily read
And it became so dear.
I found that my soul He could feed
As each word became clear.

I underlined the words God used
In all His instructions.
Each day to Him my heart was fused
Even in corrections.

Each promise from Him was for me
And mine if I would ask.
He'd answer them for me to see
That His Word was to last.

God's Word was precious and so right
And just what I needed.
I learned to keep His truths in sight
So His Word I heeded.

I'd always longed to hear God's Word
And the Scriptures to know.
I soon found out these things I heard
Would *show* the way to go.

. . .But when the wise is instructed,
he receives knowledge.
Proverbs 21:11b

Father, Your Word gives good instruction.
Amen.

6

In This Church in Grantville, PA

In this church in Grantville, PA
I painted quite a view.
It was too bad I could not stay
And see the project through.

From the time I snapped the first line
Till trees and rocks were seen,
I found that I had quite a time
With the large mountain scene.

A peaceful scene I do recall
With oils I did buy—
Some thirty-five feet on the wall,
Ten and a half feet high.

Each time a rally was held there
The visitors all knew
That this painter wanted to share
The picture as it grew.

From week to week others could see
Just how it did progress.
They didn't know how it would be.
It caused them all to guess.

I remember I worked along
And watched it to take shape.
There was many a prayer and song
As two years it did take.

Who among all these does not know that the hand of the LORD has done this?
Job 12:9

Father, may I remember that talents are from You.
Amen.

7

Years Later When I Nearly Lost

Years later when I nearly lost
My second husband too,
God made it clear there'd be a cost
And asked me if I knew.

"What answer will you give someday
For failing these two men?"
A lot against me He *could* say.
What message would I send?

I soon found out the reason why
This choice before me stood.
It seemed so plain I was to try
To make this marriage good.

In God's Word I found direction
And learned to my surprise,
That *I* needed some correction
If I was to be wise.

My husband had been gone for years
So when I next saw him,
I asked God to dispel my fears
And give us peace within.

We hoped a new start we would see
As we met each other.
I was to learn that I could be
Both a wife *and* mother.

But He said, "The things which are impossible with men are possible with God."
Luke 18:27

Father, help me remember You're always willing to help.
Amen.

8

We Had a Five-Year-Old Young Son

We had a five-year-old young son
Who needed his dad too.
For his sake I would be the one
To learn what *I* should do.

It's true that he watched everything
That I did good or bad.
How I would act I saw could bring
Some insight for the lad.

I wanted to cooperate
And help my marriage last.
My own ways I began to hate
And to forsake my past.

Obedience was hard to learn
But I found that I could see
My husband's ways although quite stern,
Would now be *good* for me.

I had to deal with rebellion
And my tongue learn to bite.
When I was silent and listened
I found him often *right.*

The Bible I began to read
And found God's peace within.
I felt He'd help my man to lead
And confidence he'd win.

All your children shall be taught by the LORD,
And great shall be the peace of your children.
Isaiah 54:13

Father, with Your help I can learn to do Your will.
Amen.

9

I Often Wanted My *Own* Way

I often wanted my *own* way.
Rebellion was still there.
I felt I had something to say
And longed to voice *my* share.

Because I had a stubborn will
It took some time to break.
I was to learn if I'd be still
Instructions I *could* take.

When God did show that He *knew* me
He would reveal my sin.
I found He cared and I'd soon see
In *how* I answered Him.

"Listen to what your mate tells you,"
God spoke to me one night.
"But he doesn't know what to do."
I felt that I was right.

The sting of Christ's hand on my cheek
Made me see I'd said wrong.
I learned that I was to be meek
So my man *could* be strong.

It's evident obedience
Should be to the letter.
I was to see that God's guidance
Would make my life better.

But He knows the way that I take; When He has tested me, I shall come forth as gold.
Job 23:10

Father, I desire to pass all Your tests.
Amen.

10

When My Husband Said, "Don't Do It"

When my husband said, "Don't do it"
I found that to obey,
Would give God freedom to use it
So He could show *His* way.

I didn't know God's will until
His Presence I had sought.
I struggled against my self-will
And things I had been taught.

I soon discovered that my life
Was not so very new.
I was to see that as a wife
I'd learn what I *should* do.

The need to love my own husband
Should start within my heart.
I sought God's help to understand
What was to be *my* part.

With peace that did come from within
I learned to be at ease.
As I left leadership to him
My husband I did please.

I was to see through my meekness
That my will God *could* tame.
I found that in my own weakness
The pow'r was in Jesus' Name.

Therefore God also has highly exalted Him
and given Him the name which is above every name.
Philippians 2:9

Father, may I find strength in Christ.
Amen.

11

I Found God's Way Was Not *My* Way

I found God's way was not *my* way
For how to get things done.
But soon I would learn it did *pay*
To not let my mouth run.

If my husband was to lead me
And the Lord to lead him,
I had a part I was to see
Or for me it was sin.

The kind of mother and wife too
God's shown for me to live.
I'm now supposed to follow through
And my allegiance give.

At times I'd called upon Christ's Name
And from Him I would hear.
He showed me His way was the same
And I found it to be clear.

In God's Word it is plainly said
My spirit should be meek.
My husband is to be my head,
His leadership to seek.

I aimed to try with all my might
So God could lead my man.
God wants me to do what's right
And with His help *I can.*

**But let it be the hidden man of the heart,
in that which is not corruptible,
even the ornament of a meek and quiet spirit,
which is in the sight of God of great price.
1 Peter 3:4 (KJV)**

**Father, I pray that I will always listen to You.
Amen.**

12

When I Think of What I've Been Through

When I think of what I've been through
I realize the love
That has guided me now to you
Is from the Lord above.

I've known some good days and some bad
In each and every test.
As Jesus always made me glad
I've found in Him my rest.

To learn the way that I should go
And trust in Him each day.
Through life I saw that God did show
My great need was to *pray*.

The great battles I had within
Was what I had to see,
Could bring control over my sin
And cause what's *best* for me.

I found sometimes I *could* believe
That I would overcome.
In time I learned I must receive
Some advice from someone.

The place that I am at right now
Has shown me God is *good.*
It is to Him I humbly bow
And live the way I should.

O LORD, be gracious to us; We have waited for You. Be their arm every morning, Our salvation also in the time of trouble.
Isaiah 33:2

Father, I am aware that I've often *needed* Your help.
Amen.

13

I'm Thankful God Plans to Use Me

I'm thankful God plans to use me
Although the way's been rough.
With stubborn will I couldn't see
I'd made the way so *tough*.

It's years ago that God did speak
Some wisdom to my heart.
It was His will I was to seek
And learn what was *my* part.

I wanted to do all His will
So on Him I did call.
I waited upon Him until
His thoughts for me would fall.

When I've asked Him His will to know,
"Be still," He sometimes said.
I've learned to trust Him and to grow
By His Word and be led.

Since God helped me to go through this
I know that I must share.
His purpose I don't want to miss
Nor His displeasure bear.

It's time to teach some women now
To love their husbands true.
An older woman now I bow,
And wisdom pass to you.

… that they admonish the young women to love their husbands, to love their children.
Titus 2:4

Father, now my desire is to share with others.
Amen.

14

Lord God, May Our Hearts Come to *Know*

Lord God, may our hearts come to *know*
That You will be enough.
It is with hope that we will grow
Through trials that are tough.

May we now see that You *do* care
To guide us through each day.
We long to *know* that You are there
And show us what to say.

Our lives to You we want to give
So that we may be sure
To see the way that we do live
Will help us to endure.

It's true You'll guide us as we try
To find what pleases You.
We are to learn You are close by
To help us our life through.

As days go by we'll start to sing
To You our *grateful praise.*
Our heartfelt love we want to bring,
And our hands we will raise.

What we have learned it's our desire
To hold onto this hope.
We pray our faith You'll set on fire
So with life we can cope.

Behold, God is my salvation; I will trust, and not be afraid: for the LORD JEHOVAH is my strength and my song. . .
Isaiah 12:2a (KJV)

Father, thank You for this assurance.
Amen.

Let the wife make the husband glad to come home,
and let him make her sorry to see him leave.

Martin Luther

Sources

Dolislager, Phyllis. *Fifty Things I Wish I Had Known Before I Turned Fifty*. Self-published, 1997, p. 29.

Mason, Mike. *The Mystery of Marriage*. Multnomah Books. 1985, p. 34

Strauss, Richard and Mary. *When Two Walk Together: Learning to Communicate Love and Acceptance in Your Marriage*. Here's Life Publishers, Inc., 1988, p. 38, 106.

Thanks to the women of Montgomery Evangelical Free Church in Belle Mead, NJ; the women of the Hawk Point Writers' Group in Washington, NJ; and the Facebook® friends who provided marriage tips for this book.

23598691R00065

Made in the USA
Columbia, SC
09 August 2018